D1526591

Blast THROUGH THE PAST!

AN INTREPID HISTORY OF EXPLORERS

Izzi Howell

W

FRANKLIN WATTS
LONDON • SYDNEY

Franklin Watts
First published in Great Britain in 2016 by The Watts Publishing Group

Copyright © The Watts Publishing Group 2016

Produced for Franklin Watts by
White-Thomson Publishing Ltd
www.wtpub.co.uk

All rights reserved.

Credits
Series Editor: Izzi Howell
Series Designer: Rocket Design (East Anglia) Ltd

The publisher would like to thank the following for permission to reproduce their pictures: Alamy/www.BibleLandPictures.com 7; Alamy/North Wind Picture Archives 8, 13, 15 (top), 18; Alamy/INTERFOTO 11 (top), 20; Alamy/Classic Image 21; Alamy/Pictorial Press Ltd 23; Corbis/Bettmann cover (top), 27 (top); Corbis/Leemage 10; Corbis/Tarker 22(bottom); Corbis 26; Corbis/Michael Pitts/ Nature Picture Library 28; iStock/lightphoto 9 (bottom); iStock/HultonArchive (bottom); iStock/GeorgiosArt 15 (bottom); Library of Congress 17, 24; Library of Congress/Ponting, Herbert George 27 (bottom); NASA 29 (top), 29 (bottom); Science Photo Library/Scott Polar Research Institute 25; Shutterstock/samantha grandy 4–5; Shutterstock/leoks 6; Shutterstock/Asta Plechaviciute 12; Shutterstock/Everett Historical 14, 19; Shutterstock/mikeledray 22 (top); Stefan Chabluk 9 (top), 31; Wikimedia/Margaret Duncan Coxhead 16.
All design elements from Shutterstock.

Every attempt has been made to clear copyright. Should there be any inadvertent omission please apply to the publisher for rectification.

ISBN 978 1 4451 4931 8

Printed in China

MIX
Paper from responsible sources
FSC® C104740
FSC
www.fsc.org

Words in **bold** appear in the glossary on pages 30 and 31.

Franklin Watts
An imprint of
Hachette Children's Group
Part of The Watts Publishing Group
Carmelite House
50 Victoria Embankment
London EC4Y 0DZ

An Hachette UK Company
www.hachette.co.uk

www.franklinwatts.co.uk

CONTENTS

INTREPID EXPLORERS THROUGH HISTORY

For thousands of years, communities around the world had little contact with each other. But over time, humans began to explore new areas and came across unfamiliar people and lands. Explorers set out across the Earth in search of knowledge, trade, land and glory.

Read on to find out what it was like to be an explorer at different moments in history and how the lives of explorers changed over time.

Hatshepsut
(Egypt) ●
1507~1457 BCE

Aristotle
(Greece) ●
384~322 BCE

This timeline shows you the names, nationalities and dates of the people mentioned in this book.

NORTH AMERICA

First European in North America

ATLANTIC OCEAN

Conquered land for Spain

SOUTH AMERICA

First leader of a trip around the world

First man to reach the South Pole

James Cameron (Canada) ●
1954~

Don Walsh (USA)
1931~

Neil Armstrong (USA)
1930~2012

Jacques Piccard (Switzerland)
1922~2008

Roald Amundsen (Norway)
1872~1928

Robert Falcon Scott (Britain)
1868~1912

Mary Kingsley (Britain)
1862~1900

Robert Peary (USA)
1856~1920

Henry Stanley (Britain)
1841~1904

4

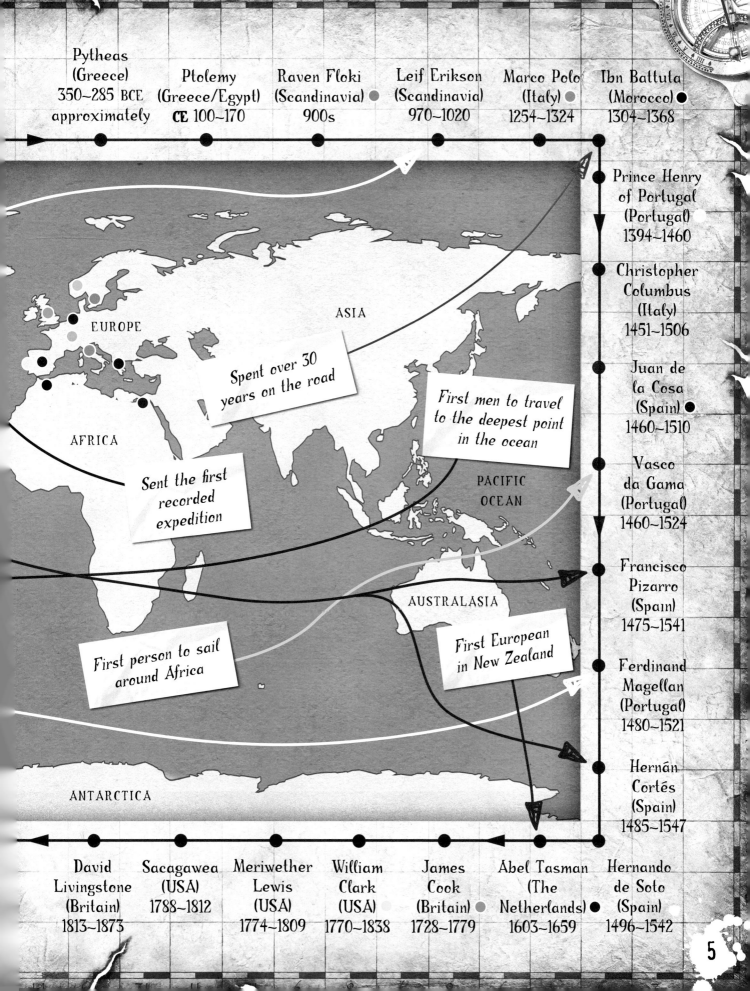

Pytheas
(Greece)
350~285 BCE
approximately

Ptolemy
(Greece/Egypt)
CE 100~170

Raven Floki
(Scandinavia)
900s

Leif Erikson
(Scandinavia)
970~1020

Marco Polo
(Italy)
1254~1324

Ibn Battuta
(Morocco)
1304~1368

Prince Henry
of Portugal
(Portugal)
1394~1460

Christopher
Columbus
(Italy)
1451~1506

Juan de
la Cosa
(Spain)
1460~1510

Vasco
da Gama
(Portugal)
1460~1524

Francisco
Pizarro
(Spain)
1475~1541

Ferdinand
Magellan
(Portugal)
1480~1521

Hernán
Cortés
(Spain)
1485~1547

ASIA

EUROPE

Spent over 30
years on the road

First men to travel
to the deepest point
in the ocean

AFRICA

PACIFIC
OCEAN

Sent the first
recorded
expedition

Vasco
da Gama
(Portugal)
1460~1524

AUSTRALASIA

First person to sail
around Africa

First European
in New Zealand

ANTARCTICA

David
Livingstone
(Britain)
1813~1873

Sacagawea
(USA)
1788~1812

Meriwether
Lewis
(USA)
1774~1809

William
Clark
(USA)
1770~1838

James
Cook
(Britain)
1728~1779

Abel Tasman
(The
Netherlands)
1603~1659

Hernando
de Soto
(Spain)
1496~1542

5

ANCIENT ADVENTURES

The ancient **Egyptians, Greeks** and **Phoenicians** sailed round every inch of the Mediterranean coastline, looking for new lands to **settle** and new people to trade with.

Gold →

Terrific traders

Some commonly traded items were purely practical, such as tin from northern Europe. Others were just for fun, such as ivory and **incense** from Africa. The female Egyptian **pharaoh**, Hatshepsut, became more powerful by sending out trading expeditions. She sent five ships of **slaves** on a mega trading trip to East Africa in 1470 BCE to fetch gold, ebony and exotic furs.

HAVE YOU GOT WHAT IT TAKES?

NAVIGATOR

PERSONALITY PROFILE: Sun gazer

The Sun was a seriously useful **navigation** tool for ancient explorers, as it always rises in the east and sets in the west. Explorers could work out the position of north and south by the shadows cast by the Sun.

Ancient Egyptian wooden trading boats were rowed by slaves.

Ivory →

The brainy ancient Greeks weren't just interested in trading — they also travelled to learn more about science and geography. The Greek philosopher Aristotle noticed that the stars in Egypt were in a different position in the sky than they were in Greece. This helped him realise that the Earth was round. Up until this point, most people thought that it was flat. The geographer Ptolemy used his knowledge of maths to add lines of **latitude** and **longitude** to his maps.

EPIC EXPLORERS

NAME: Pytheas (Approximately 350 BCE to 285 BCE)

NATIONALITY: Greek

KNOWN FOR: Telling tales

ACHIEVEMENTS: When Pytheas returned from sailing around Britain, no one believed his tales of a mixture of land, sea and air that felt like a jellyfish! Today we know that Pytheas was sort of telling the truth — he was actually describing sheet ice.

Ptolemy created one of the first maps of the world in the 2nd century CE.

VIKING VOYAGES

The **Vikings** were super sailors and shipbuilders. They sailed from Scandinavia across northern Europe and Britain to raid and trade, reaching as far east as Turkey!

Bigger and bigger

Viking voyagers set out from Scandinavia in search of new lands, where they could settle and grow food. Some sailed far across the Atlantic Ocean and found Iceland, Greenland and the mysterious Vinland.

You'd better not come back!

Raven Floki releasing his birds.

HAVE YOU GOT WHAT IT TAKES?
RAVEN WRANGLER

PERSONALITY PROFILE: Eagle-eyed

When out at sea, the Viking explorer Raven Floki would release ravens as a way of testing if they were close to land. The ravens would come back to the ship if they didn't see land. When one raven didn't return, Floki followed it and ended up in Iceland!

Viking explorers were up for an adventure. After hearing rumours of land to the west of Greenland, one explorer named Leif Erikson set off with a crew of 35 men to see what was there. Lucky Leif landed on the east coast of the continent of North America, 500 years before Christopher Columbus (see pp.14–15). He named the land Vinland.

see pp.14–15

MUST BE ABLE TO:
navigate a knorr

Strong ocean storms could destroy small ships, so the Vikings used sturdy knorrs for long voyages. Unfortunately, knorrs were too heavy to be rowed, so they were powered by a single sail. Fingers crossed for wind!

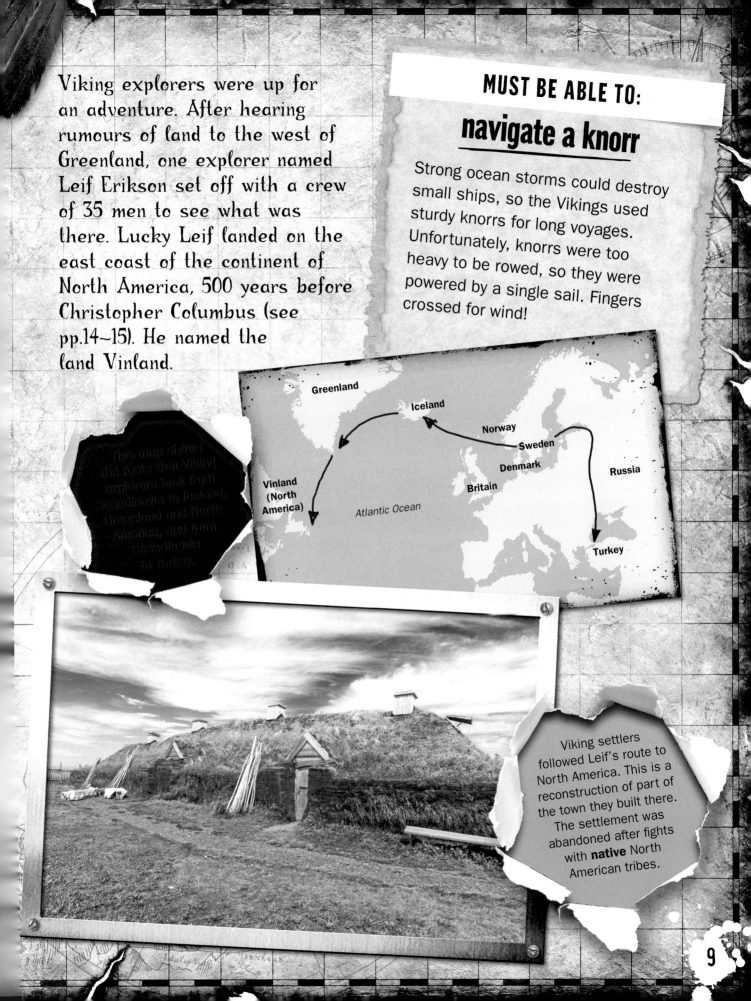

This map shows the route that Viking explorers took from Scandinavia to Iceland, Greenland and North America, and from Scandinavia to Turkey.

Greenland

Iceland

Norway

Sweden

Denmark

Russia

Vinland (North America)

Britain

Atlantic Ocean

Turkey

Viking settlers followed Leif's route to North America. This is a reconstruction of part of the town they built there. The settlement was abandoned after fights with **native** North American tribes.

SILK ROAD SIGHTSEEING

In the early **Middle Ages**, objects that were hard to find in Europe, such as silk and spices, travelled with traders and explorers along the Silk Road – an overland trading route between China, India and Europe.

Exploring the empires

The Silk Road went through the **Islamic** and the **Mongol empires**. These empires tried to protect travellers carrying valuable goods against robbers. Despite the risks, **Muslim** explorers, such as Ibn Battuta, and friends of the Mongols, such as Marco Polo, safely travelled long distances.

Dates ➡️

HAVE YOU GOT WHAT IT TAKES?
CAMEL CARER

TOP SKILL: Holding onto a hump

Explorers and traders rode camels across the deserts and mountains of the Silk Road, as the camels could carry heavy loads and it was too tiring to walk in the heat. To keep their camels happy and healthy, explorers travelled at a slow speed and carried camel snacks, such as dates.

Travellers rode along the Silk Road in large groups known as **caravans**.

NAME: Ibn Battuta (1304-1368)

NATIONALITY: Moroccan

AKA: Muslim mega-explorer

ACHIEVEMENTS: Ibn Battuta was on the road for over 30 years exploring the Islamic Empire and beyond, both alone and as part of a caravan. He travelled at least 120,000 kilometres around Africa, Asia and Europe, making him one of the greatest explorers of all time.

HE SAID WHAT?

'Never travel the same road twice.'

Ibn Battuta knew not to waste time repeating cities or countries – he always had his eye out for his next adventure!

Ibn Battuta's route

NAME: Marco Polo (1254-1324)

NATIONALITY: Italian

AKA: Mate of the Mongols

ACHIEVEMENTS: Marco Polo travelled along the Silk Road to China with his father and uncle, before spending 24 years exploring Asia and running errands for his friend Kublai Khan, the head of the Mongol Empire. When he returned to Italy, many thought that his tales seemed too wild to be true, but they did inspire a young boy named Christopher Columbus (see p.15).

THE AGE OF DISCOVERY

In the 15th century, Prince Henry of Portugal got bitten by the exploring bug. He footed the bill for research into superior ships and new ways to navigate. Sailors practised their skills on trips around the Atlantic Ocean and along the West African coast. The Age of Discovery had begun!

Prince Henry →

Caravel

Portuguese progress

Portuguese navigational know~it~alls developed new tools to measure latitude at sea. Early expeditions into the Atlantic Ocean helped sailors to understand and use ocean winds and currents to their advantage. Engineers invented light and speedy triangular~sailed caravel ships, which could sail into the wind along shallow coasts and across deep oceans, unlike most ships, which sail with the wind behind them.

This modern statue in Lisbon, Portugal, features important Portuguese explorers and inventions.

Countries such as Spain were worried by Portugal's exploration expertise, and jealous of the gold they were gaining from trade with West Africa. They didn't want to miss out on claiming new land or discovering quicker **trade routes** to Asia, so they sent out explorers to see what they could find.

Magellan's Spanish crew were angry about taking orders from a Portuguese leader, but Magellan succesfully dealt with a **mutiny** during his trip.

MUST BE ABLE TO:

find a rich sponsor

Ships and supplies weren't cheap, so explorers needed rich countries to **sponsor** their trips. The competition between European countries meant that if an explorer's first choice of country didn't want to cough up the cash, they could always try to persuade another country! The Portuguese explorer Ferdinand Magellan was sponsored by Spain on his trip to **circumnavigate** the Earth.

ASIA OR BUST

15th century sailors and traders were desperate to find an easier way to bring back pricey spices from Asia to Europe. Travelling by land was slow and dangerous, so explorers set out to find a better sailing route around the world.

East or west?

Portugal's Vasco da Gama was the first European to sail to India by going around southern Africa. Unaware that there were two continents in the way, Christopher Columbus thought it would be quicker to sail west to Asia instead, and stumbled across the islands of the Bahamas in North America.

I asked you to bring me pepper, not people!

While Columbus didn't get to stock up on spices, he did bring back gifts of native slaves, corn and pineapples for the Spanish royal family.

Corn ➡

It wasn't enough for 15th century explorers to simply discover new lands – they also kept charts and drew maps so that they could make their way back there!

The Spanish **cartographer** Juan de la Cosa drew maps of newly discovered lands, such as this map from 1500 of North and South America.

HAVE YOU GOT WHAT IT TAKES?
NAVIGATOR

MUST HAVE ITEM: A log

To measure the speed that they were moving at, explorers such as Columbus threw a log on a string over the edge of the boat. They guessed the speed of the ship based on the time it took for it to move away from the log.

EPIC EXPLORERS

NAME: Christopher Columbus (1451-1506)

NATIONALITY: Italian

KNOWN FOR: Continent confusion

ACHIEVEMENTS: Christopher Columbus arrived in what he believed to be India (the region would later become known as the West Indies) in 1492. Even though he'd got the continent wrong, Columbus's journey inspired a huge wave of Spanish and Portuguese explorers that led to the conquest of South America.

HE SAID WHAT?

'For the execution of the voyage to the Indies, I did not make use of intelligence, mathematics or maps.'

Navigation of an unknown route was quite hit and miss, so Columbus relied heavily on good luck to get him to his destination, rather than skill!

CRAFTY CONQUISTADORS

Columbus's voyages inspired Spanish explorers to make the trip west for themselves. Many settled in the Caribbean for several years, before moving down into Central and South America when they heard rumours of gold and unimaginable wealth.

Across the Americas

The first European explorers of Central America had to battle through jungles and swamps. It was easier for later Spanish explorers, such as Francisco Pizarro, to make their way through the **Inca** empire in Peru with its network of paved roads! Over time, the Spanish explorers started to **seize** land and kill native people. They became known as conquistadors, or conquerors.

In battle, the native people of South America were unprepared to fight against conquistadors in metal armour on horseback.

HAVE YOU GOT WHAT IT TAKES?
HORSE RIDER

TOP SKILL: Rapid riding

There were no horses in the Americas before the Spanish arrived, so conquistadors brought their own! Conquistadors could travel much faster on horseback than on foot, which gave them the upper hand in battle over the native South Americans, who fought on foot.

The conquistadors weren't very interested in saving the culture and traditions of the native South Americans. Their main aims were to spread the **Catholic** religion and to grab as much gold as possible! Later, huge numbers of people came over from Spain to settle in South America.

HAVE YOU GOT WHAT IT TAKES?
* REPORT WRITER *

PERSONALITY PROFILE: Big boaster

King Carlos I of Spain would give the conquistadors money and land if they sent him reports about their good progress claiming land and gaining control of native people. When the king heard that the Spanish conquistador Hernán Cortés had helped destroy the Aztec empire, he made him governor of Mexico.

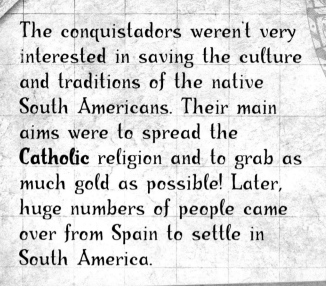

Seems like a nice chap...

The **Aztec** emperor Montezuma welcomed Cortés in Mexico, not knowing that his arrival would eventually break apart the Aztec empire.

Hernán Cortés at your service sir.

RIVERS
AND RATIONS

Still searching for gold, the Spanish started to explore North America in the 16th century. Later, French and British explorers unsuccesfully looked for a northern land route to the Pacific Ocean. Eventually, American explorers, Lewis and Clark, travelled by river from the middle of the country to the Pacific Ocean in the 19th century.

Two's company...

Safety in numbers didn't work out well for the explorers that chose to travel in large groups. The crowds of unfamiliar men immediately caught the eye of native North American tribes, who knew every inch of their territory. Explorers who travelled alone seemed less scary to local tribes.

native North American warriors

When Spanish explorer Hernando de Soto and his large army arrived at the Mississippi River, they were immediately met by native North American warriors in canoes.

Hernando de Soto

HAVE YOU GOT WHAT IT TAKES?
DIPLOMAT

PERSONALITY PROFILE: Good guest

On their trip searching for a river route across the USA, Lewis and Clark stayed in the good books of native North American tribes by bringing them gifts of knives and beads. Lewis and Clark's other secret **diplomatic** weapon was a native North American woman, Sacagawea. Her knowledge of native languages helped Lewis and Clark to deal with hostile tribes.

An explorer's relationship with native North American tribes could make or break their expedition. If the native North Americans felt safe and respected, they would help explorers find food and give them supplies. If explorers treated them badly, it could be the end of their trip and their lives!

HAVE YOU GOT WHAT IT TAKES?
CHEF

MUST BE ABLE TO COOK:
"Portable soup"

Urgggh!

Lewis and Clark knew that it could be tricky to find food on their trip, so they brought along portable soup just in case! Portable soup was a thick paste, made by boiling beef, eggs and vegetables. Just add water for instant soup!

Portable soup

Sacagawea

I'm pretty sure there was a river around here somewhere...

Lewis and Clark travelled with around 30 people, including Sacagawea, her husband and her baby.

DOWN UNDER

In the late 16th century, Spanish ships regularly crossed the Pacific Ocean, trading back and forth between the Spanish-controlled countries of Mexico and the Philippines. However, the huge size of the Pacific meant that these ships rarely saw new lands, unless they were blown off course by the wind.

Sailing south

By the 17th century, explorers from Britain, France and the Netherlands had begun to sail around the South Pacific, keen to find spices to trade and mythical lands rumoured to be filled with gold. Their voyages led them to real countries, such as New Zealand.

Tasman's ship was attacked by Maori warriors in canoes. Four of Tasman's men died in the attack.

EPIC EXPLORERS

NAME: Abel Tasman (1603-1659)

NATIONALITY: Dutch (the Netherlands)

KNOWN FOR: Moaning about the Maori

ACHIEVEMENTS: Although Tasman was the first European to discover New Zealand and Tasmania, he refused to explore the islands after his ship was attacked by the native Maori people of New Zealand. Tasman went on to explore more of the South Pacific, but he never went back to New Zealand!

HAVE YOU GOT WHAT IT TAKES?
NAVIGATOR

MUST HAVE ITEM: A clock

18th century explorers often had navigational problems because the **pendulum** clocks that they used to work out longitude didn't work well on rough seas. The 18th century British explorer James Cook was one of the first explorers to use a clockwork clock, which wasn't affected by movement. This made his navigation and mapping of the Pacific much easier.

James Cook was one of the first explorers to map and take an interest in Australia. After a shipwreck forced his crew to spend several weeks on the east coast of Australia, the **naturalist** Joseph Banks studied the fascinating local animals and plants while Cook claimed the land for Britain.

MUST BE ABLE TO:
stomach pickled cabbage

Sailors lived in fear of scurvy – a horrible disease in which your gums bleed, old wounds open, and you eventually die! To stop his crew from getting scurvy, Cook stocked his ship with Vitamin C-rich carrot jam and pickled cabbage for them to eat on their trip.

Pretty birds Mr Banks.

Indeed Cookie ...er, Captain.

Cook and Banks observed many types of Australian wildlife. When they arrived back in Britain, Banks' drawings got Europe interested in life down under.

ACROSS AFRICA

European explorers often sailed along the coastline of Africa but they didn't head inland until the late 19th century. Many explorers were put off exploring Africa by its sweltering deserts, fierce animals and deadly diseases.

Go with the flow

Some explorers, such as David Livingstone, wanted to find a river route across Africa, so that people could transport items for trade more easily. At the time, many European and Arab traders worked along the coast of Africa, selling native people as slaves. Livingstone hoped that the slave trade would end if traders could make more money from trading objects across Africa along river routes.

MUST BE ABLE TO:

look cool in a pith helmet

To keep cool in the hot tropical sun, explorers wore hats made from pith (the spongy part of the stem of a plant). In a time before suncream, the wide brim of the hat kept their pale skin from getting burnt!

Livingstone explored the Ruzizi River in central Africa with the British explorer, Henry Stanley.

Although some explorers wanted to learn about the geography and people of Africa, many explorers had money and power on their minds. When explorers reported that Africa was rich in valuable gold, diamonds and rubber, European countries took control of the people that lived there and stole the riches for themselves.

HAVE YOU GOT WHAT IT TAKES?
ANIMAL TAMER

PERSONALITY PROFILE:
Wildlife wary

Knowing how to handle African wildlife was a matter of life or death for explorers. After a hungry lion munched on Livingstone's arm, he was left disabled for life. Other explorers were luckier – Mary Kingsley calmed down an angry hippo by scratching it behind its ear with her umbrella!

SHE SAID WHAT?

'You have no right to go about Africa in things you would be ashamed to be seen in at home.'

Mary Kingsley became well known for travelling across Africa wearing the same clothes that Victorian women wore in Britain.

I'm perfectly comfortable, thank you!

Mary Kingsley in a typical exploring outfit

EPIC EXPLORERS

NAME: Mary Kingsley (1862–1900)

NATIONALITY: British

KNOWN FOR: Wandering alone through West Africa

ACHIEVEMENTS: At a time when women were expected to stay at home with their families, Mary Kingsley set off alone to explore West Africa. She visited tribes, canoed up rivers and climbed a 4 km-high mountain, before writing two books about the importance of saving traditional African cultures.

POLES APART

Explorers had tried to reach the poles before, but without strong boats to cut through the thick ocean ice, many expeditions got stuck, and had to turn back. Some explorers even died, trapped in their ships without enough food.

> I may look daft, but I'm toasty!

Breaking through

By the early 20th century, advances in shipbuilding meant that boats could travel through the polar ice without getting stuck. Rich countries started taking an interest in these unexplored places and many governments paid for expensive expeditions. For the first time in history, polar explorers had a good shot at getting to the poles.

The American explorer Robert Peary wore animal furs to keep warm in sub-zero temperatures.

With no one else around at the isolated poles, explorers had to do everything for themselves, from washing their smelly socks to fixing complicated machinery. Polar explorers needed some serious skills.

Stewed penguin

HAVE YOU GOT WHAT IT TAKES?

NAVIGATOR

PERSONALITY PROFILE:

Maths genius

Take one totally white landscape, add in a touch of snow blindness, and it's a recipe for disaster! Although shipbuilding technology had advanced, navigation hadn't quite caught up. Without calculators or GPS, explorers did complicated mental arithmetic and used equipment such as **sextants** to avoid getting lost.

Do you mind!

MUST BE ABLE TO:

cook stewed penguin

Polar explorers ate a whopping 7,000 calories a day to stay alive. Finding food in the icy poles was a challenge, so explorers had to get creative! At the British base camp in Antarctica, stewed penguin and curried seal were on the menu, but away from camp, explorers had to make do with pemmican (ground meat mixed with fat).

This stuff stinks Bert!

Chefs at the base camp used seal blubber as fuel for their stove!

ON THIN ICE

The biggest rivals in the race to the poles were Robert Falcon Scott and Roald Amundsen. Both men set off for the South Pole towards the end of 1911, but only one could get there first.

In a rush

Scott – already a hero from an earlier expedition to Antarctica – was keen to hang on to his fame. Amundsen originally had his heart set on the North Pole, but Robert Peary claimed to have got there first in April 1909. Amundsen refused to miss out again, and just beat Scott to the South Pole.

HAVE YOU GOT WHAT IT TAKES?
SLED DRIVER

TOP SKILL: Husky handling

Huskies' warm fur and stamina made them the top choice for Amundsen. Scott experimented with ponies, but ended up having to pull the sleds by hand after all his ponies died!

MUST BE ABLE TO:
work wonders with a screwdriver

When you're marching through a blizzard, every gram of weight matters! Polar explorers DIY-ed their equipment to be as light as possible. Amundsen's team slimmed down their sledges to one third of their original weight.

Some of Amundsen's huskies have a well-earned rest at the South Pole.

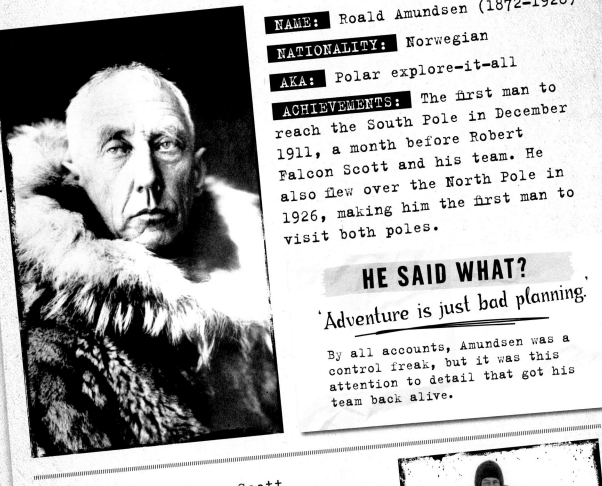

NAME: Roald Amundsen (1872–1928)

NATIONALITY: Norwegian

AKA: Polar explore-it-all

ACHIEVEMENTS: The first man to reach the South Pole in December 1911, a month before Robert Falcon Scott and his team. He also flew over the North Pole in 1926, making him the first man to visit both poles.

HE SAID WHAT?

'Adventure is just bad planning.'

By all accounts, Amundsen was a control freak, but it was this attention to detail that got his team back alive.

NAME: Robert Falcon Scott (1868–1912)

NATIONALITY: British

AKA: Mr Unlucky

ACHIEVEMENTS: After months of bad weather, the loss of sled-pulling ponies and stretched supply lines, Scott experienced the ultimate let-down when he found Amundsen's Norwegian flag already flying at the South Pole. Sadly, Scott and his team died on their way back to base camp.

FINAL FRONTIERS

In the past 100 years, we have started to explore what lies deep below the ocean waves and far above our planet. New designs of **submersibles** and spacecraft can take us deeper and higher than ever before.

Deep down

When **sonar** was developed to find enemy submarines in the First World War (1914–1918), it opened our eyes to the mysterious 10,994 km–deep Challenger Deep in the Pacific Ocean. American Don Walsh and Swiss Jacques Piccard first reached the bottom in 1960. Today, modern submersibles allow explorers to take films of the depths and grab samples with a hydraulic arm.

HE SAID WHAT?

'It's really the sense of isolation... realizing how tiny you are down in this big vast black unknown, and unexplored place.'

As the only person in the Deepsea Challenger submersible, it's easy to understand how Canadian explorer and *Avatar* film director James Cameron felt alone at nearly 11,000 kilometres from the water's surface.

This type of submersible is used by scientists to explore shallow water.

The unmanned *Voyager 1* spacecraft has now left our solar system and is heading further into space.

Far out

Space exploration has rocketed out of this world in the past 50 years. Solar powered technology now allows spacecraft to stay in space permanently, and manned trips to other planets, such as Mars, are being planned. New generations of explorers will go even further than *Voyager 1* and make amazing new discoveries in the years to come.

EPIC EXPLORERS

NAME: Neil Armstrong (1930-2012)

NATIONALITY: American

AKA: Number one moonwalker

ACHIEVEMENTS: After a long competition with the Russians to be the first to send a man to the Moon, Neil Armstrong sealed the deal for the USA when he took 'one small step for a man, one giant leap for mankind' on the Moon in 1969.

GLOSSARY

BCE – The letters BCE stand for 'before common era'. They refer to dates before the year CE 1.

CE – The letters CE stand for 'common era'. They refer to dates after the year CE 1.

caravan – a group of people travelling across a desert together

cartographer – someone who makes or draws maps

Catholic – a Christian religion that has the Pope as its leader

circumnavigate – to sail all the way around something

diplomat – someone whose job it is to keep a good relationship between groups of people

empire – a group of countries ruled over by one country

incense – something that is burned to create a strong sweet smell

latitude – the distance north or south you are from the Earth's equator

longitude – the distance east or west you are from the Greenwich meridian

Middle Ages – a period of time between the 12th and the 15th century

Muslim – describes someone who believes in the religion of Islam

mutiny – when a group of people refuse to obey orders because they want to be in control themselves

native – describes the people who lived in a country first

naturalist – someone who studies animals and plants

navigation – to find the right direction to travel by using maps and other equipment

pendulum – a heavy object on a chain that moves from side to side inside a clock

pharaoh – a ruler in ancient Egypt

seize – to take something

settle – to start living in a place where you are going to live for a long time

sextant – a tool used for measuring angles in order to discover the exact position of an object

slave – someone who is owned by someone else and has to work for them

sonar – a system, used especially on ships and submarines, which uses sound waves to find the position of things in the water

sponsor – to pay for someone else to do an activity

submersible – a boat that can travel underwater for research or exploration

trade route – a long route used by people buying and selling goods

ANCIENT CIVILISATIONS

VIKINGS
(CE 700–1100)
– a group of people originally from Scandinavia that conquered land across northern Europe, creating a Viking empire.

EGYPTIANS
(3100–30 BCE)
– a civilisation based around the River Nile in Egypt, which was ruled by a pharaoh.

GREEKS
(750–30 BCE)
– an advanced Mediterranean civilisation that studied science, maths and medicine.

PHOENICIANS
(1500–150 BCE)
– a shipbuilding civilisation that came from modern-day Lebanon and settled along the Mediterranean coast.

Viking settlements
Egyptians
Greeks
Phoenicians
Aztecs
Inca
Islamic Empire
Mongols

AZTECS
(CE 1100–1521) – a group of people that ruled over most of Mexico and Central America before the arrival of the conquistadors.

INCA
(CE 1438–1572)
– a civilisation that grew along the west coast of South America and was eventually destroyed by Spanish conquistadors.

ISLAMIC EMPIRE
(CE 622–1250)
– a vast area across Europe, Africa and Asia that followed Muslim laws and was originally part of a single empire.

MONGOLS
(CE 1206–1335)
– an empire that stretched from Central Europe to Japan, which was created by Genghis Khan.

INDEX

Further information

http://www.bbc.co.uk/schools/
primaryhistory/famouspeople/
christopher_columbus/

Sail Christopher Columbus's ship across the Atlantic and learn more about his life.

http://www.spacekids.co.uk/spacehistory/

See a timeline of space exploration and learn how humans have explored space.

http://www.nationalgeographic.com/
125/timelines/women-explorers/

Find out about female explorers throughout history.

Every effort has been made by the Publishers to ensure that the websites in this book are suitable for children, that they are of the highest educational value, and that they contain no inappropriate or offensive material. However, because of the nature of the Internet, it is impossible to guarantee that the contents of these sites will not be altered. We strongly advise that Internet access is supervised by a responsible adult.